GLOBAL MARKET OF PHYSIOTHERAPY

Physical therapy services provide a cost-effective way to prevent short-term disabilities from becoming chronic conditions, to help avoid invasive procedures, to speed recovery from surgery and musculoskeletal injuries and to eliminate or minimize the need for opioids.

This is a fragmented but growing $34 billion per year industry of small physical therapy clinics, and a few large chains. Demand is growing due to an aging population, ongoing sports injuries, joint replacement surgeries, rising obesity

BEST WAYS TO GROW YOUR PHYSIOTHERAPY PRACTICE

levels, and the cost savings and effectiveness of outpatient rehab.

Here are some things to know about this healthcare sector:

- **Physical therapy market size:** Market data estimates that the U.S. physical and occupational therapy industry was worth $34.5 billion in 2018, up 6.2% from 2017. The total market is forecast to grow at a 6.2% average annual pace, to $45.7 billion by 2023. Revenue growth has been steady since 2007.

- **Number of physical therapy clinics in the U.S.:** There are an estimated 38,800 clinics in America providing physical therapy, occupational therapy, speech therapy and audiology. Average annual receipts per clinic are $886,000, and they have a 14.6% net profit margin.

- **Market drivers:** Early hospital discharge practices foster greater demand for outpatient physical therapy services, and PT clinics believe that their therapy services provide a cost-effective way to prevent short-term disabilities from becoming chronic conditions.

- **Competitive landscape:** This industry has been consolidating for 10+ years, yet private practice remains very fragmented. The 20 largest companies—two public operators and eight private equity-backed operations—captured just 21 percent of the industry's market share. The potential for "roll-ups" is high.

- **Sources of revenue in the physical therapy industry:** The principal sources of payment for the clinics' services are managed care programs, commercial health insurance, Medicare/Medicaid and workers' compensation insurance.

- **Physical therapy salary and job growth:** Physical therapists earned an average of $79,850 in 2017, and projections by the Labor Dept.

reveal that physical therapists are expected to see job growth of 28% through 2024. The median pay for occupational therapists was $84,270 in 2018, and job growth is expected to increase 27% from 2014 through 2024.

- **Number of physical therapy companies:** There were 24,342 physical therapy companies or firms operating in the United States in 2012. Of this tally, 94.2% were single-unit operations that captured 54% of industry receipts.

SOURCE:MARKETRE SEARCH.COM{A BLOG BY JOHN LAROSA}

GROWTH OF INDIAN PHYSIOTHERAPY MARKET

According to recently published Pharmaion report, "**India Physiotherapy Equipment Market Opportunities, 2010 - 2020**", the physiotherapy equipment market in India is projected to grow at a CAGR of over 12% during 2015 - 2020, on account of increasing prevalence of cardiovascular and neurological diseases, expanding elderly population and escalating demand for at-home physiotherapy. Moreover, growing awareness about the therapeutic benefits of physiotherapy such as improving mobility and strengthening affected body areas is significantly propelling demand for physiotherapy equipment in India.

Market Research and Market Trends of Physiotherapy services Ecosystem

- Physiotherapy started from simple massage and is nowadays available in wide range of therapies with many specialized applications. In the past, physiotherapists were not always recognized as a contributing member of a hospital care team. Therapy plans were developed and administered later in the cycle of care. Modifications in rules, mainly driven by the Affordable Care Act, have given Physical Therapists their rightful role as an influential member of the care team. Nowadays has become widely accepted as a treatment therapy after any major/minor accident or even after recovery for ill health. They help in limiting assistance from devices like crutches, braces, canes, splints etc. Typically it costs about 300-400 USD for such a treatment.

- With the growing geriatric population number of accidents such as elderly falls in household and outdoors will rise also the malfunctioning of joints has become common these days, will rise further which would lead to an obvious surge in the need for physiotherapists and advanced techniques like aquatic therapy designed for patients with low pain tolerance . The accidents may be due to natural cause such as calamities or due to personal mistakes of individuals or groups. Performance of hospitals these days is evaluated on basis of patient readmission rates, and physiotherapists are finally being recognized as key contributors to the care transition process from hospital to outpatient or home services. Physiotherapists are involved in preparing patients for transition and are being relied upon to provide input and strategies for how physical therapy can help reduce avoidable 30-day readmission rates.

- The progress in preventive techniques like yoga and preventive medicine is expected to be a growth restraint for these services. There are surgeries for same complete replacement of malfunctioning part also. Direct access and autonomous practice of physical therapy is not as simple but the interface between patient and physiotherapist is expected to become more simpler by the implication of technology such as mobile applications suggesting exercises and alarming on the right times to perform them.

- Other health services will also prosper so there is expected to be a competition among physiotherapists and other health professionals. But the advent of methods like hydrotherapy and electrotherapy would pose a serious competition. There is not much development at present in measurement of degree of treatment of physiotherapy but growing modernization will ultimately lead to measurable outcomes for these treatments also. Equipment for tilting, bending, stretching, etc. is already available to assist physiotherapists.

- Physiotherapists are naturally a creative and resourceful group of care providers, so it is no surprise that many are now incorporating the use of video games aided by virtual reality (VR) into their treatment plans. Implication of techniques by using platforms such as the Nintendo Wii, allows therapists to take advantage of the motion-sensitive controllers to drive patients to perform targeted movements. Wii-Hab approach is proving to be a way to engage patients in actively participating in their recovery and allow treatment to expand beyond the clinical setting.

Patients who enjoy the process of recovery are more likely to stick to it.

What is marketing?

The action or business of promoting and selling products or services, including market research and advertising to the target audience.

What is promotion?

Promotion means spreading information about an product, service or issue. **Promotion** as part of marketing means spreading information about a product, product line, brand, or company. **Promotion** includes: Publicity and public relations, Advertising.

So promotion and marketing is not the same thing. A small part of marketing is called promotion. But this 2 are the main pillars of any business or service or product.

THE 7 PILLERS OF MARKETING.

EVERY PROFESSIONAL SHOULD KNOW THIS ELEMENTS OF MAEKETING TO SELL HIS OR HER PRODUCT OR SERVICE.THIS ARE AS FOLLOWS---

1. PRODUCT

2. PRICE

3. PLACE.

4. PROMOTION.

5. PEOPLE

6. PHYSICAL EVIDENCE

6. PROCESS

1. Product:

The service product requires consideration of the range of services provided, the quality of services provided and the level of services provided. Attention will also need to be given to matters like the use of branding, warranties and after-sale service. The service product mix of such elements can vary considerably and may be seen in comparisons of service range between a small local building society and one of the largest in the country; or between a small hotel offering a limited menu range and a four star hotel offering a wide range of meals.

2. Price:

Price considerations include levels of prices, discounts allowances and commissions, terms of payment and credit. Price may also pay a part in differentiating one service from another and therefore the customers perceptions of value obtained from a service and the interaction of price and quality are important considerations in many service price sub mixes.

3. Place:

The location of the service providers and their accessibility are important factors in services marketing. Accessibility relates not just too physical accessibility but to other means of communication and contact. Thus the types of distribution channels used (e.g. travel agents) and their coverage is linked to the crucial issue of service accessibility.

4. Promotion:

Promotion includes the various methods of communicating with markets whether through advertising, personal selling activities, sales promotion activities and other direct forms of publicity, and indirect forms of communication like public relations.

Expanded mix for services:

Because services are usually produced and consumed simultaneously, customers are often present in the firm's factory, interact directly with the firm's personnel, and are actually part of the service production process. Also, because services are intangible customers will often be looking for any tangible cue to help them understand the nature of the service experience.

These facts have led services marketers to conclude that they can use additional variables to communicate with and satisfy their customers. For example, in the hotel industry the design and decor of the hotel as well as the appearance and attitudes of its employees will influence

BEST WAYS TO GROW YOUR PHYSIOTHERAPY PRACTICE

customer perceptions and experience.

Acknowledgment of the importance of these additional communication variables has led services marketers to adopt the concept of an expanded marketing mix for services. In addition to the traditional four Ps, the services marketing mix includes people, physical evidence, and process.

5. People:

All human actors who play a part in service delivery and thus influence the buyer's perceptions: namely, the firm's personnel, the customer, and other customers in the service environment. All of the human actors participating in the delivery of a service provide clues to the customer regarding the nature of the service itself. How these people are dressed, their personal appearance their attitudes and behaviors all influence the costumers perceptions of the service.

The service provider or contact person can be very important. In fact, for some services, such as consulting, counseling, teaching, and other professional relationship – based services, the provider is the services. In other cases the contact person may play what appears to be a relatively small part in service delivery, for instance, a telephone installer, an airline baggage handler, or an equipment delivery dispatcher. Yet research suggests that even these providers may be the focal point of service encounters that can prove critical for the organization.

6. Physical Evidence:

The environment in which the service is delivered and where the firm and customer interact, and any tangible components that facilitate performance or communication of the service. The physical evidence of service includes all of the tangible representations of the services – such as brochures, letterhead, business cards, report formats, signage, and equipment. In some cases it includes the physical facility where the service is offered, for example, the retail bank branch facility.

In other cases, such as telecommunication services, the physical facility maybe irrelevant...In this case other tangibles such as billing statements and appearance of the repair truck may be important indicators of quality. Especially when consumers have little on which to judge the actual quality of service they will rely on these cues just as they rely on the cues provided by the people and the service process. Physical evidence cues provide excellent opportunities for the firm to send consistent and strong messages regarding the organization's purpose, the intended market segments, and the nature of the service.

7. Process:

The actual procedures, mechanism and flow of activities by which, the service is delivered the service delivery and operating systems. The actual delivery steps the customer experiences, or the operational flow of the service, will also provide customers with evidence on which to judge the service.

Some services are very complex, requiring the customer to follow a complicated and extensive series of actions to complete the process. Highly bureaucratized services frequently follow this pattern, and the logic of the steps involved often escapes the customer.

Another distinguishing characteristic of the process that can provide evidence to the customer is whether the service follows a production-line/standardized approach or whether the process is an empowered/customized one. None of these characteristics of the service is inherently better or worse than another.

Rather, the point is that these process characteristics are another form of evidence used by the consumer to judge service. For example, two successful airline companies, Southwest in the United States and Singapore Airlines, follow extremely different process models. Southwest is no-frills (no food, no assigned seats), no exceptions, low-priced airline that offers frequent, relatively short length domestic flights.

All of the evidence it provides is consistent with its vision and market position. Singapore Airlines, on the other hand, focuses on the business traveler and is concerned with meeting individual traveler needs. Thus, its process is highly customized to the individual, and employees are empowered to provide nonstandard service when needed. Both airlines have been very successful.

The three new marketing-mix elements (people, physical evidence, and process) are included in the marketing mix as separate elements because they are within the control of the firm and any or all of them may influence the customer's initial decision to purchase a service, as well as the customer's level of satisfaction and repurchase decisions.

Certainly Marketing managers in services markets need to undertake research about the markets and market segments for which their respective marketing mixes are shaped. Wherever possible the services marketing manager will need to research and analyses the characteristics of the markets served. It is these problems of conducting such analysis and research that we now examine

WHY EVERY PROFESSIONAL SHOULD KNOW ABOUT MARKETING TO BECOME SUCCESSFUL----

I WILL TRY POINT WISE EXPLANATION FOR THIS

1. CUSTOMER SATISFACTION

2. CORPORATE IMAGE

3. COMPETITIVE ADVANTAGE

4. EXPANSION OF BUSINESS

5. BRAND LOYALTY

6. ORGANISATIONAL OBJECTIVE

7. OPTIMUM UTILIZATION OF RESOURCES

8. EFFICIENCY

CUSTOMER SATISFACTION

CUSTOMER SATISFACTION IS THE OUTCOME OF A CORRELATION BETWEEN PRODUCT PERFORMANCE (PP) AND CUSTOMER EXPECTATION (CE).

WHEN PP MATCHES WITH CE, THE CUSTOMER WILL BE <u>SATISFIED</u>.

WHEN PP BELOW THAN CE, THE CUSTOMER WILL BE DESSATISFIED.

WHEN PP EXCEEDS CE, THE CUSTOMER WILL BE DELIGHTED.

WHEN PP EXCEEDS VERY MUCH THAN CE, THE CUSTOMER WILL BE ASTONISHED.

CORPORATE IMAGE

MARKETING HELPES A PROFESSIONAL TO DEVELOP AND ENHANCE ITS

BEST WAYS TO GROW YOUR PHYSIOTHERAPY PRACTICE

CORPORATE OR BRAND IMAGE.WITH THE HELP OF EFFECTIVE MARKETING A PROFESSIONAL CAN ACHIEVES HIGHER PERFORMANCE. SUCH AS INCREASE IN SALES AND PROFIT.

COMPETITIVE ADVENTAGE

EFFECTIVE MARKETING HELPES TO FACE COMPETITION IN THE MARKET.COMPETITION IS A MUST HAPPEN PROCESS IN THE ON GOING BUSINESS SECTORS WHICH MAY BE ANY THING ,SUCH AS HEALTHCARE SECTORS TO MANUFACTURERS.PROFESSIONAL MARKETERS ARE PROACTIVE IN ANY

BEST WAYS TO GROW YOUR PHYSIOTHERAPY PRACTICE

DECISION MAKING.THEY COME UP WITH----

I. INNOVATIVE DESIGNS OR MODELS

II. CREATIVE PROMOTIONS SCHEMES

III. EFFECTIVE CUSTOMER RELATIONSHIP TECHNIQUES

EXPANSION OF BUSINESS

EFFECTIVE MARKETING IMPROVES THE PERFORMANCE OF ANY BUSINESS WICH IN TURN HELPS TO GROW THE BUSINESS.FOR BUSINESS EXPANSION ONE MAY

BEST WAYS TO GROW YOUR PHYSIOTHERAPY PRACTICE

UNDERTAKE VARIOUS ACTIVITIES LIKE---

I. MARKET PENETRATION

II. MARKET DEVELOPMENT

III. PRODUCT DEVELOPMENT

BRAND LOYALITY

IT MEANS

I. REPEAT PURCHASES BY SATISFIED CUSTOMERS

II. RECOMMENDATIONS BY EXISTING CUSTOMERS TO FRIENDS AND OTHERS

ORGANISATIONAL OBJECTIVES

MARKETING HELPS ANY ONE TO BUILD SOME OBJECTIVES WHICH ARE

I. HOW TO INCREASE IN PROFIT

II. HOW TO INCREASE IN SALES

III. HOW TO INCREASE IN BRAND LOYALITY AND IMAGE

OPTIMUM UTILIZATION OF RESOURCES

DUE TO PROPER MARKETING, THE COMPANY OR ANY PEROFESSIONAL GET HIGHER DEMAND FOR GOODS OR

SERVICES. INCREASE IN DEMAND LEADS TO HIGHER DISTRIBUTION OR PROFIT. SO ANY PROFESSIONAL OR COMPANY SHOULD MAKE AN OPTIMUM USEG OF CAPITAL RESOURCES, MANPOWER RESOURSES, PHYSICAL RESOURCES. MISMANAGEMENT OF THIS FACTORS CAN DESTROY ANY BUSINESS

EFFICENCY

AS MARKETING BRINGS HIGHER PROFITES, A PART OF THE PROFIT SHOULD

BE SPENT ON VARIOUS ACTIVITIES SUCH AS---

I. CONTINUE RESEARCH AND DEVELOPMENT

II. TECHNOLOGY OR EQUIPMENTS UPGRADATIONS

III. TRAINING AND DEVELOPMENT

THIS FACTORS ARE VERY MUCH ESSENTIAL FOR GROWING A BUSSINESS

SO WE DISCUSSED ABOUT THE BASIC LEVEL IMPORTANCE OF EFFECTIVE MARKETING TO GROW ANY BUSINESS.PLEASE UNDERSTAND THIS FACTORS BEFORE GOING TO NEXT CHAPTAR.

BEST WAYS TO GROW YOUR PHYSIOTHERAPY PRACTICE

CHAPTER 2

NOW I WILL DESCRIBE THE VERY IMPORTANT DO AND DON'T TO BE A SUCCESSFUL PHYSICAL THERAPIST FROM EVERY WAY THAT IS- FAME,PROFIT,PATIENT SATISFACTIONS AND RETENTION.DO REMEMBER PHYSICAL THERAPY IS NOBEL HEALTH CARE PROFESSIONAL SO YOU MUST LEARN IT IN A SERIOUS MANNER THEN ONLY YOU CAN EXICUTE THE STRATAGIES IN YOUR

BEST WAYS TO GROW YOUR PHYSIOTHERAPY PRACTICE

PRACTICE TO BRING GROWTH IN IT.

THE FOLLOWING IDEAS CAN CHANGE YOU AND YOUR PRACTICE FOREVER. FIRST I WILL DISCUSS THE THINGS THAT MUST BE DONE OR INCLUDED IN PRACTICE.

1. DO FACTOR 1--

FIRST QUESTION YOURSELF WHAT IS USP?

THE FULL FORM OF USP IN MARKETING IS UNIQUE SELLING PROPOSITION. YOUR USP MEANS HOW YOU

PRACTICE? HOW YOU APPROACH PATIENTS? HOW YOU ARE DIFFERENT FROM OTHER THERAPISTS IN TOWN?

DON'T BE THE SAME, BE BETTER.

FOR EXAMPLE, YOU HAVE TO PROVIDE SOMETHING EXTRA AND UNIQUE TO THE PATIENTS FOR BETTER BUSINESS.

SOME IDEAS WHICH CAN INCREASE YOUR USP-

I. YOU ARE THE ONLY PHYSIO TO PROVIDE IASTM THEARPY

II. YOU ARE THE ONY PHYSIO WHO PROVIDES SOME SPECIAL PROCEDURES LIKE YOGA OR COUNSELING OR OSTEOPATHY OR OBESITY MANAGEMENT etc TO YOUR PATIENTS WHICH OTHERS CAN NOT PROVIDE.

ASK YOURSELF, WHAT UNIQUE YOU CAN PROVIDE TO YOUR CLIENTS.

PLEASE DO NOT SKIP THIS FORMULA. WITH OUT THIS ALL OF YOUR INVESTED AMOUNT IN ADVERTISEMENT OR

MARKETING CAN BE WASTED.SO TRY TO INCREASE YOUR USP AS MUCH AS YOU CAN BECAUSE USP IS DIRECTLY PROPERTIONAL TO YOUR PROFIT.

2. DO FACTOR 2—

PREPARE A SUATABLE LOGO FOR YOUR SERVICES AND CLINICS.THIS WILL PROVIDE YOU A GOOD BRANDING.DESIGN THE LOGO IN SUCH A MANNER THAT IT EXPRESS SOME UNIQUE THINGS ABOUT YOUE AND YOUR CHOICE.DO ALL THE

MARKETING UNDER THIS LOGO.

LOGO HELPS YOU TO LOOK LIKE A PROFESSIONAL TRUSTWORTHY BUSINESS WHICH WILL GIVE YOU MORE PATIENTS

3. DO FACTOR3—

CREAT SPECIAL OFFERS WITH YOUR TREATMENT PACKAGE.ITS VERY GOOD IDEA TO BRING YOU IN THE LIME LIGHT IN YOUR TOWN.YOU DON'T HAVR TO GIVE CONCESSIONS IN YOUR PROFESSIONAL FEES.JUST PROVIDE SOME EXTRA SERVICE WHICH

YOU KNOW BETTER, FOR EXAMPLE-

: FREE MIGRAINE SCREENING

: FREE KETO DIET ADVICE TO CONTROLE WEIGHT

: FREE BALANCE AND FALL RISK ASSESSMENT

: FREE NEUROPATHY ASSESSMENT IN DIABETICS

HIGHLIGHT ALL THIS TYPES OF OFFERS IN YOUR MARKETING POSTCARDS,BANNERS,DIGITAL MARKETING PLATFORMS,ETC.

THIS WILL DEFINITELY ATTRACT NEW PATIENTS.BUT AGAIN ASK YOURSELF WHAT UNIQUE FREE SERVICE YOU CAN PROVIDE WITH YOUR PAID TREATMENT

4. DO FACTOR 4—

PAIN IS THING THAT BRINGS ABOUT 80% OF YOUR TOTAL PATIENTS IN A YEAR.WHEN PAIN STARTS PATIENTS THINKS ABOUT PHYSICAL THERAPY BECAUSE NOW A DAYS PEOPLES ARE AWEAR OF THE POTENTIAL SIDE EFFECTS OF PAIN

KILLERS.IN THIS FAST AND DIGITAL LIFESTYLE ANBODY OF ANY AGE CAN GET MUSCULOSKELETAL PAIN ANY TIME OF THE YEAR.

SO YOU HAVE TO THINK ABOUT MAKING EFFECTIVE MARKETING THROUGH OUT THE YEAR,NOT FOR 2 TO 3 MONTHS.YOU HAVE TO BE IN TOP OF MIND OF PEOPLES THROUGH OUT THE YEAR.THEN ONLY THEY WILL SEE YOU IN THEIR FIRST ATTEMPT.THUS YOU CAN MAKE A GOOD FLOW OF NEW PATIENTS AND PATIENT RETENTION.

BEST WAYS TO GROW YOUR PHYSIOTHERAPY PRACTICE

THE WAY HOW YOU DO IT IS DEPENDS UPON YOU AND YOUR LOCALITY.YOU CAN MAIL OR CREAT FREE SOCIAL MEDIA POST IN A REGULAR INTERVAL.ASK YPUR SELF ABOUT SUITABLE METHOD YOU CAN ADOPT ACCORDING TO YOUR POTENTIAL.

5. DO FACTOR 5--

ACCORDING TO STATISTICS, DIRECT MAIL MARKETING IS THE MOST PREFERRED FORM OF MRKETING.

Check out these statistics:

BEST WAYS TO GROW YOUR PHYSIOTHERAPY PRACTICE

- Direct mail produces up to **500% more responses** than all other marketing methods. (DMA 2015 Response Rate Report)
- **92% of consumers prefer direct mail** when looking to buy a product. (DMA 2015 Response Rate Report)
- The *average* return on investment (ROI) for direct mail marketing is **18%-20%.** (DMA 2015 Response Rate Report)

BUT YOU SHOULD KEEP IN MIND THAT A SINGLE POSTCARD DESIGN WILL NOT HELP YOU.MAKE MINIMUM 12 DESIGNS WITH DIFFERENT OFFERS, NEW TREATMENTS, And NEW PACKAGES.AND YOU HAVE TO FOCOUS ON

EVERY GROUP OF POPULATION. YOUR CONTACT DETAILS SHOULD BE WELL MENTIONED THERE.

6. DO FACTOR 6—

IN THIS DIGITAL ERA YOU MUST NAIL YOUR SELF IN EVERY PLAT FORMS AVAILABEL WHICH MAY BE FREE OR PAID. ONE THING KEEP IN MIND ALWAYS YOU SHOUD BE IN TOP OF

BEST WAYS TO GROW YOUR PHYSIOTHERAPY PRACTICE

THE PRIORITY LIST ALWAYS BY ANY MEANS BECAUSE NO BODY WILL GIVE A DAMN SPACE WITHOUT FIGHT.SO TRY ALL THE MEANS BY WHICH YOU CAN REACH CLIENTS AND RETAIN THEM FOR NEXT ISSUE.

HERE IS SOME IDEAS WHER YOU CAN GO DIGITAL

: FIRST OF ALL MAKE YOUR PERSONAL WESITE WITH ALL POSSIBLE REAL PICTURES, VIDEOS,POSTCARDS,LIVE CHAT,AUTO MAILING,CONACTS,ETC.

DON'T FORGET TO USE POP UPS WICH MUST CONTAIN THE SPECIAL EYE CATCHY OFFERS CREATED BY YOU ONLY.

: ENLIST YOURSELY IN POPULAR SEARCHING WEBSITES AND APPS LIKE GOOGLE MY BUSINESS, JUSTDIAL, LYBRATE, PRACTO, INDIAMART, GOOGLE AD SENSE, ETC. IF POSSIBLE USE SEARCH ENGINE OPTIMIZATION(SEO) TO IMPROVE GOOGLE RANKING.

: USE FACEBOOK, WHATSAPP, AND

INSTAGRAM ETC PLATFORMS.

POST INTERESTING PICTUTERS, VIDEOS, QUOTS REGARDING YOUR TREATMENT PROTOCOLD OR CLINICS

IN ONE LINE YOU'RE ONLINE PRESENCE MATTERS VERY MUCH, BUT NO PERSONAL POST, ONLY YOUR BUSINESS RELATED POSTS.

7. DO FACTOR 7—

PRINT MARKETING ALSO PLAYS A VERY BIG ROLE IN EFFECTIVE

MARKETING.ALWAYS REMEMBER THAT YOUR PATIENTS ARE THE BIGGEST GOLD MINE YOU ARE SITTING ON.SO TO ALWAYS KEEP IN TOUCH WITH THEM EVEN IF THEIR TREATMENT IS OVER.IF THER RECOVERED FROM YOUR HAND THEN THEY WILL BE FAN OF YOU AND REFER MANY OTHER NEW PATIENTS TO YOU.

PRINT SMALL NEWSLETTERS ABOUT DISEASES,NEW TREATMENTS AVAILABEL IN YOUR CLINIC,YOUR OFFERS,YOUR ACADEMIC

UPGRADATION DETAILS WITH PICTURES,ETC.IT WILL DEFINITELY BOOST DIRECT AND REFERAL PATIENTS FLOW.

8. DO FACT 8--

THE DESIGN OF YOUR CLINIC IS ONE OF THE KEY FEATURES OF YOUR BUSINESS AND YOUR UNIQUE IDENTITY.

DESIGN YOUR CLINIC IN SUCH A WAY THAT PATIENTS FEEL VERY MUCH COMFORTABLE DURING TREATMENT SESSIONS.FOR THIS YOU SHOULD DESIGN YOUR TREATMENT PLINTH

SCINTIFICALLY,ESURE PRIVACY OF EACH AND EVERY PATIENTS,ALL MODERN EQUPMENTS SHOULD BE AVAILABE LIKE DIGITAL OR WHITE MARKER BOARD,ANATOMICAL MODELS OF SEVERAL JOINTS TO DEMONSTRATE THE PATIENTS PROBLEM ACCORDING TO THEIR WAY.

INSTADE OF SIMPLY DEMONTRATING SOME EXERCISE, PROVIDE INSTANT PRINTOUTS OF THAT WHICH WILL BE TAGGED BY YOUR LOGO OR BRANDING.

YOU CAN START AN AWARNESS CHANNEL IN YOUTUBE OR WRITE BLOGS ON TRENDING TOPICS.LIVE IN THE POCKET OF PATIENT, MEANS IN THE MOBILE.

9. DO FACTOR 9—

CONSTANTLY WORK ON YOURSELY REGARDING YOUR PROFESSIONAL SKILLS, KNOWLEDGE,

AVAIL ALL TYPES OF ADVANCED EQUIPMENTS IN YOUR SIDE.

ATTAIN ALL POSSIBLE CME, WORKSHOP,

CONFERANCES AND POST THEM IN YOUR DIGITAL PLATFORMS OR NEWSLETTERS.

10. DO FACTOR 10—

PATIENT RETENTION POLICY IS VERY CRUCIAL THING TO UNDERSTAND.YOU SHOULD KNOW THIS TOOL PROPERLY.

IF ONE PATIENT COME TO YOU FOR KNEE PAIN AND TAKE 15 SITTINGS,MAKE SURE BY YOUR ELIGIBILITY THAT SAME PATIENT SHOULD COME TO YOU AGAIN AFTER

6MONTHS OR 1 YEAR WITH ANOTHER PROBLEM OR ISSUE.IF HE OR SHE DOES NOT CAME BUT THEY MAY REFER PATIENTS TO YOUR CLINIC.IN BOTH WAY THIS IS PATIENT RETENTION. THE ENTIRE THING I HAVE MENTIONED BEFORE, ARE THE KEY TO YOUR SUCCESSFUL PATIENT RETENTION POLICY. FEW THIGS WILL BE ADD UP LIKE YOUR BEHAVIOUR, YOUR SKILL, YOUR PREVIOUS WORKING HISTORY AND GOOD RATING IN YOUR ONLINE AND OFFLINE PATIENTS TESTIMONEALS.

YOU CAN MAKE A TESTIMONIAL OR FEEDBACK FORM FOR PATIENTS AND ASK PATIENTS AT END OF TREATMENT TO PROVIDE INFORMATION ABOUT HIS OR HER SATISFACTION LEVEL. THIS IS HOW YOU CAN IMPROVE YOURSEL FORM THE PATIENTS VIEV, ETC.

LET'S ELABORATE A TOPIC CALLED PATIENT RETENTATION,

WHAT IS THE VALUE OF PHYSICAL THERAPY PATIENT RETENTION?

Attracting new patients to your physical therapy clinic is probably at the top of your list for marketing efforts. After all, new patients represent new business and that means more revenue. When you started your physical therapy practice, you had to find a way to attract new patients, and you have probably continued using the same methods.

What about making an effort to retain the patients you have?

You made the effort to bring them in the first place, but are you doing all you can to get the most benefit out of them? If not, some of your marketing budget is being wasted.

It actually costs more to attract new patients than it does to retain current patients. You have to spend time and money educating potential patients about what you do, the services you offer and how you are different from other physical therapy clinics. The up-front investment in time and money to establish a new patient can be great.

Efforts to retain an existing patient, however, can be much more cost-effective. Current patients already know who you are and what you do. They have already benefited from your services. Make the most out of their positive experience, and your current patient could become a long-time patient. They can also bring in other new patients through word of mouth or a referral program with less effort on your part. A satisfied patient who remains with your physical therapy clinic for the long term has the opportunity to bring in several new patients over time. When consumers find something they like, they want to share it with others around them who may benefit. Whether your loyal patient is a rehabbing athlete or a Baby Boomer recovering from joint replacement surgery, they know other people in similar situations.

Each of your current patients is part of a demographic that fits your ideal client base. Allowing your patients to act as brand ambassadors for your clinic cuts out the cost of identifying and reaching your target demographic.

When you have a group of loyal customers, you have a strong fan base for your physical therapy clinic. Loyal customers like to interact with other patients via online reviews and other organic promotions.
Approximately **<u>27% of social media users</u>** post health-related status updates. Think

healthcares institutions regularly participate in social media, especially on Face book. At least 26% of hospitals have a presence on social media, sharing information with patients, educating the public and extending their relationships with patients. Patients are adapting to interacting with their healthcare providers via the Internet.

Your regular patients gathering on social media also become a free vehicle for your marketing communications. When you let your fan base know about a new service you are offering, they spread the word for you. They are also more likely to try your new service themselves.

Retaining patients for your physical therapy clinic has several advantages over attracting new patients. Although it is important to do both, here are some ideas for physical therapy patient retention methods.

DECREASE PHYSICAL THERAPY PATIENT CHURN RATE

Your patient churn rate is the percentage of patients who drop out before they have completed the recommended number of physical therapy sessions. We know that patients who do not complete their course of treatment are more likely to experience less-than-optimum results. Regardless of the quality of care you provide them, patients who are not satisfied with the outcome will blame the physical therapy clinic.

According to a recent study published by Strive Labs, approximately **70% of patients drop out of physical therapy before they have attended the recommended number of sessions**. That is a lot of potentially unsatisfied customers. By keeping these patients engaged long enough to complete their recommended course of therapy, you can increase positive outcomes and build a bigger fan base.

Start by calculating the churn rate at your physical therapy clinic. For each patient, identify the number of sessions attended and divide that by the number of sessions recommended. Multiply that number by 100 to get the churn rate for each patient expressed as a percentage. Average all of your patient percentages together to see the churn rate for your entire practice.

Tracking your churn rate will help you see if the efforts you are making to retain patients are working. The lower your churn rate, the better your patient retention. Here are some tips for decreasing your patient churn rate

- Start with a great first impression. Many people are intimidated by physical therapy because they have no experience with it, and most of your patients come to therapy with pain that can severely affect their mental outlook. Make sure each patient gets a fantastic first impression of your clinic. You want them to feel comfortable and hopeful that you are going to make them feel better.

- **Offer superior care.** Exceeding patient expectations is a great way to keep them coming back. This means managing their expectations from the beginning and then providing a better outcome.
- **Understand your competition.** Physical therapy clinics have become popular in the last decade. You are probably not the only option for your patients' treatment. Learn what your competitors offer and what you can do to stand out.
- **Be a good listener.** You are the expert, but it is the

patient who is experiencing the pain. Recognize that there is an emotional component to physical disability, even if it is only temporary. Getting your patients to feel that someone is listening to them and genuinely wants to help will allow you to develop a better rapport.

- **Teach your patients.** The more patients know about their physical therapy treatments, the more compliant they will be. Explain some of the theory behind what you are doing and how it is going to help your patient overcome their condition.

- **Build loyalty.** When your patients arrive for their appointments, let them know you were expecting them and have prepared for their session. Make them feel like an important part of your day. Make them feel like you are working with them as a team and their participation is vital.
- **Identify drop out risks early.** For "at risk" patients, early intervention is key. Take note of behaviors that suggest a lack of commitment to the process or a disinterest in the outcome. You'll want to work harder to make a personal connection with

these patients to keep them coming back.
- Find out why patients drop out. Use some type of exit interview to determine why patients stop coming to physical therapy before their course of treatment is completed. This information will help you make changes that will increase your retention rate.
- Offer alternative modalities. Offering different modality types provides options to patients who have difficulty using one modality type. It also creates variety for those who become tired of

repetitive exercises. Many patients become more motivated and positive when they can see results using different types of therapy, such as aquatic therapy, where they can move with less pain and will be more likely to continue therapy.

- **Start with a great first impression.** Many people are intimidated by physical therapy because they have no experience with it, and most of your patients come to therapy with pain that can severely affect their mental outlook. Make

sure each patient gets a fantastic first impression of your clinic. You want them to feel comfortable and hopeful that you are going to make them feel better.
- **Offer superior care.** Exceeding patient expectations is a great way to keep them coming back. This means managing their expectations from the beginning and then providing a better outcome.
- **Understand your competition.** Physical therapy clinics have become popular in the last decade. You are probably not the only

option for your patients' treatment. Learn what your competitors offer and what you can do to stand out.
- **Be a good listener. You are the expert, but it is the patient who is experiencing the pain. Recognize that there is an emotional component to physical disability, even if it is only temporary. Getting your patients to feel that someone is listening to them and genuinely wants to help will allow you to develop a better rapport.**
- **Teach your patients.** The more patients know about their physical therapy treatments, the more

compliant they will be. Explain some of the theory behind what you are doing and how it is going to help your patient overcome their condition.
- **Build loyalty.** When your patients arrive for their appointments, let them know you were expecting them and have prepared for their session. Make them feel like an important part of your day. Make them feel like you are working with them as a team and their participation is vital.
- **Identify drop out risks early.** For "at risk" patients, early intervention is key. Take note of behaviors that

suggest a lack of commitment to the process or a disinterest in the outcome. You'll want to work harder to make a personal connection with these patients to keep them coming back.
- **Find out why patients drop out.** Use some type of exit interview to determine why patients stop coming to physical therapy before their course of treatment is completed. This information will help you make changes that will increase your retention rate.
- **Offer alternative modalities.** Offering different modality types

provides options to patients who have difficulty using one modality type. It also creates variety for those who become tired of repetitive exercises. Many patients become more motivated and positive when they can see results using different types of therapy, such as aquatic therapy, where they can move with less pain and will be more likely to continue therapy.

EDUCATE YOUR PATIENTS

Many patients come to physical therapy without a clear understanding of what you can do for them. They may have a script from their doctor and a complaint of pain or lack of mobility, but they don't truly understand how physical therapy works. In their minds, it is like medication: The doctor writes the prescription, and they come to you to fill it.

It is up to you to educate your patients about the full range of services you provide and the benefits to building a healthy lifestyle, including regular physical therapy. You need to explain to them how different treatment modalities work and the potential outcomes that are available for their acute issue. But then, they need to know about the long-term benefits you can provide with land-based therapy, aquatic therapy and other modalities.

You want your patients to see physical therapy as not just an answer to their acute needs, but also as a tool to promote ongoing health, mobility, pain management and injury prevention. By educating your patients on all the services you offer, you can help them understand why building a lasting relationship with you would be a great benefit.

Some methods you could use to educate your patients include:

- **Send out a regular newsletter.** A newsletter

that contains news about your practice and the industry in general keeps your practice top of mind for your patients. You could include notes about new services you provide, new research results for your treatment modalities and incentives you offer to encourage patients to refer a friend. Getting a newsletter will help remind your patients about your physical therapy clinic and open their eyes to different ways people use your services.

- **Personal phone calls to check in with past patients.** People like a personal touch, especially when it comes to healthcare. Call your patients one week after they complete a round of therapy to ask how they are doing. You can suggest options if they are having some follow up issues and tell them about other services they could benefit from.

- **Have printed materials handy.** Take-home resources like brochures and pamphlets that explain the services you provide are a good reinforcement for the information you tell your patients. It will help them to be able to review the information at home after their visit, and people tend to give more credibility to information that is put in writing.

- **Give advance information.** People who are new to physical therapy may be apprehensive. Providing them with information about how to prepare for their visit will ease their tension. Educating patients on what to do, wear, bring and expect in their first therapy session can make them feel comfortable and more likely to embrace adding physical therapy to their lifestyle.

Making these efforts to educate your patients will help them feel cared for. When they sense you are concerned about their well-being, they are more likely to want to develop and continue a relationship with your practice.

DON'T FACTORS

HERE I WILL DISCUSS ABOUT COMMON MISTAKES AND RED FLAGS FOR A PHYSIOTHERAPIST.

ALL YOU HAVE CONSIDER THE BELOW FACTORS,,,,

1. DO NOT TREAT A PATIENT WITHOUT PROPER LISTING TO THE PATIENTS FULL COMPLAINS

2. DONT BE DISHONEST WITH YOUR PATIENT

3. DONT BE THE KING OF EGO. MANY PATIENTS DON'T LIKE THIS.

4. TRY TO LEARN ABOUT THE GREVENCE MANAGEMENT OF PATIENTS

5. DO NOT MAKE YOUR PRACTICE INDECIPLINED.

www.ingramcontent.com/pod-product-compliance
Lightning Source LLC
Chambersburg PA
CBHW020603220526
45463CB00006B/2432